PARTIALLY EXCITED STATES

WISCONSIN POETRY SERIES

RONALD WALLACE, *Series Editor*

Charles Hood

PARTIALLY EXCITED STATES

THE UNIVERSITY OF WISCONSIN PRESS

Publication of this volume has been made possible, in part, through support from the Brittingham Fund.

The University of Wisconsin Press

1930 Monroe Street, 3rd Floor
Madison, Wisconsin 53711-2059
uwpress.wisc.edu

3 Henrietta Street, Covent Garden
London WC2E 8LU, United Kingdom
eurospanbookstore.com

Printed in the United States of America

This book may be available in a digital edition.

Library of Congress Cataloging-in-Publication Data

Names: Hood, Charles, 1959– author.
Title: Partially excited states / Charles Hood.
Other titles: Wisconsin poetry series.
Description: Madison, Wisconsin : The University of
             Wisconsin Press, [2017] | Series: Wisconsin
             poetry series | Includes bibliographical references.
Identifiers: LCCN 2016041566 | ISBN 9780299311643 (pbk. :
             alk. paper)
Subjects: | LCGFT: Poetry.
Classification: LCC PS3558.O538 P37 2017 | DDC 811/.54—
             dc23 LC record available at
             https://lccn.loc.gov/2016041566

CONTENTS

Invisible Terrain

The History of Hell in America

Escape Velocity

ACKNOWLEDGMENTS

Thank you to the Playa Foundation, the Center for Art + Environment at the Nevada Museum of Art, the Annenberg Community Beach House, and the Center for Land Use Interpretation for fellowships and residencies that helped make this book possible.

Thank you also to the editors and journals kind enough to publish me: *Catamaran*, *Chautauqua*, *The Crunge*, *Diagram*, *Los Angeles Review*, *New England Review Digital*, and *Santa Monica Review*. Alternate versions of "Pelt Vault, National History Museum" and "Magazine Tiger, *Harper's Bazaar*" appeared in a limited-edition, accordion-fold chapbook, *25 Tigers*, illustrated by Christine Mugnolo and released by Colibri Press. "All Males Die after Mating" is reprinted by permission of *Chautauqua*, © 2015 by Charles Hood.

1

Invisible Terrain

*After seeing these pictures you end up finally not knowing
any more whether a jukebox is sadder than a coffin.*

—JACK KEROUAC, INTRODUCTION TO *THE AMERICANS*

The Wand Chooses the Wizard

the same way the gat chooses the thug
the shiv chooses the stoodge,
the baton chooses the policeman
and the arrow chooses the saint.

No, the wand chooses the wizard
while the patsy chooses the mark
and the floozy chooses the lug,
Manischewitz chooses the wino

and the trailer park chooses the tornado
FEMA will take two years to process.
Even now, the town looks like a cartoon
prizefighter missing half his teeth.

The wand chooses the wizard in Afghanistan
while the .338 Lapua Magnum B408 bullet
capable of a confirmed kill at 2,707 yards
chooses the sniper. The new surfboard

chooses the ten-year-old and the ten-year-old,
now in his twenties, about to win the Gold Coast
Pro Surfing Contest in Australia, chooses
the shark. No, the book chooses the reader

the way the brook chooses the fisherman,
the triple axel chooses the skater,
the Vera Wang dress chooses the bride.
The husband waits, choosing silk boxers.

The book is tired of you now,
has chosen somebody else.
You will never know how it ends.
The wand chooses the wizard

but this poem has chosen you, only you,
and it is still choosing you, even now.
This poem was always going to pick you
and it will never change its mind.

How My Parents Died

I finally get to Montana—I have always wanted to go to Montana—
but while I am there, my parents die. Great, now I have to go home

and take orphan lessons. *Cause of death* asks the nicely dressed lady
at the dead person certification office. She has a form. *What will be*

cause of death? Would it cost more to say that they died skydiving—
yes, that is closest to the facts: we will say they were stunt doubles

in the next James Bond movie. What if it were a dual suicide by stoning?
I think the truth is, Father died in Tibet, on a dinosaur dig, while Mother

died of a broken heart after signing 100 petitions for Amnesty International.
What about the whales, I ask the lady, the whales gone deaf because of sonar

Navy tests? Can we mention whales at the funeral? My folks were run over
by a movie star who in turn was fleeing from photographers. It is okay;

they had been bitten by rabid bats just before, so were doomed anyway.
Concussions from surfing too close to the reef. Poisoned by raw oysters

at a Malibu orgy. Hit by falling stars. Trampled by zebras while bareback,
after climbing the fence at the zoo, a fence that says CAUTION: WILD ZEBRAS.

All right then, we'll tell the truth. My parents died when I told them they
were adopted, they were not my real parents, I got them from an agency

in China. I had always made sure to love them the same, I told them, but
it was too late: the shock was too much. My parents died when they had sex

with Zeus without their sunglasses or their medication. My parents died reading
Moby-Dick aloud to blind children at the foster care agency; after the final page,

they both spontaneously burst into flames. I have their ashes here now
in this Tupperware, along with the smoke-singed copy they were reading.

I will bury it all at the Mount of Olives. I will dig and dig, make a deep hole,
deep enough for all of us—I will spade it square and clean and when done

I will climb into it and pull the dirt over me like a blanket.

Bois de Boulogne

Dear Committee Members: Please consider my application to be the next artist-in-residence, Bois de Boulogne. From my studies I know a great deal about Bois de Boulogne. I know that five new specimens of ribbon worms from Bois de Boulogne will arrive soon. That a pelting of meteorites just pitted the western margins of the Bois de Boulogne. That a fireball streaked through the sky and that the buried lakes of Bois de Boulogne are actually connected to one another. That the air temperature in Bois de Boulogne is rising three times faster and that in fifteen years the seven glaciers in Bois de Boulogne have increased their outgassing tenfold. From the *New York Times*: in Bois de Boulogne, an unknown species of colossal squid was caught off the coast of Bois de Boulogne. I know that until recently China had been planning to export dissidents to Bois de Boulogne if Marseilles hadn't first invaded New Zealand, which broke away from Bois de Boulogne and shattered. That the cloud that has formed each year over Bois de Boulogne resembles the face of the New York man with a gun who said to the pilot, Fly me to Bois de Boulogne. That the AP reports a Galápagos penguin was recently recovered in Bois de Boulogne, lost, and entomologists just described a new fly, *Scaptia beyonceae*, from Bois de Boulogne's closest-to-Paris pissoirs. I know that the five-story-tall Rodin Glacier spews blood-red waterfalls. That the Neutrino Observatory tracks blue flashes it hopes will signify meaning. A tree called the monkey penis tree only blossoms once every one hundred years and smells like vanilla and rotting beef. *Modern Painters* now covers Bois de Boulogne, and an art-themed water park was built to celebrate. Many animals flee to Bois de Boulogne. A cruise ship in Bois de Boulogne was stuck in the fog with two hundred tourists aboard. They were airlifted to Bois de Boulogne. The State Department once considered sending their marked-for-death Vietnamese collaborators to live out their days in cottages in the Bois de Boulogne. When the question arises of Manet, Proust, Renoir, what did they know of Bois de Boulogne, the answer is always the same: nothing. I own a detailed topographical survey map of the secret rivers of Bois de Boulogne; in Moscow I have seen the circus that casts monkeys as pilgrims whose promised land is Bois de Boulogne. Scientists have identified a kind of singing iceberg grounded in the lakes of Bois de Boulogne. When you sent Werner Herzog to make his film, the committee said he deserves to live and die in Bois de Boulogne, and that it deserves him, in return. The leading cause of death is not the damp, tubercular chill, but suicide, which is why red parkas should be worn daily. Please, sirs, I long to wear the parkas of Bois de Boulogne; this is why I plan to write a ten-hour opera about how red is the redness of Bois de Boulogne. If I were dying I would want just one thing: to be allowed to die painting in the Bois de Boulogne. There are no better chestnuts, no better plane trees than these. Committee Members: you should know that each of my children is named Bois de Boulogne. Everything before now that I ever wrote about love, really was about Bois de Boulogne. Members, you may think that you already know the Bois de Boulogne, but until you let me undress her for you and carve a statue of Bois de Boulogne out of blood and travertine, you will never understand the true frostbitten, gangrenous, impossible meaning of radioactive, lava-scalded, tree-filled Bois de Boulogne.

The Invention of Punctuation

The semicolon is older than the fork, true
or false, while the em dash predates stirrups

in warfare. To see ellipsis points well drag
an old sofa to the end of a pier, push it off,

count the spirals of bubbles. Who remembers
the exclamation point, vivid as a neon condom?

Finger quotes can only be used by "experts."
The ampersand looks like a man tying a shoe

without sitting down first, but not so good in academia
because it feels so much like Marlon Brando shouting

Stella in a wife-beater. What does the period do?
The period shuts the door, turns out the lights.

It teaches us to be firm but not bossy, the parent
in charge even during tantrums, square-jawed

and resolute. In German, *Der Punkt,* a good name
for a punk band—no, a good name for anything,

full stop. Commas blink in the sunlight, so take a break,
go easy, these stairs just go up and up, don't they?

At the top we can rest on a bench in the shade. The view
of the tile roofs makes it look like a painting of Provence.

Shutters: worn sills: an attic garret. The camera
dollies closer. Starlings scatter then reflock.

We can see a man in a white shirt sitting at a desk
in a plank-floored, white-walled room, fingers

resting on the keyboard of a mechanical typewriter.
Paper glows in a small stack beside him. August's

storm clouds purple the horizon, promising
if it has not rained yet, it will soon. The man

finishes his drink and gets up to rinse the cup
and sits back down and then lifts both hands

and begins to type.

State Insects

Butterflies, for example:
California has the Dogface

that feeds on False Indigo
or any purple flower.

Baltimore Checkerspot holds
Maryland's place in the list;

Kentucky simmers with Viceroys.
The Zebra Longwing in Florida

is well named, its aposematic stripes
warning blue jays and stray dogs

not to lick. Maybe it will rain
and I can be a ladybug

(state mascot of Delaware,
Massachusetts, New Hampshire,

North Dakota, Ohio,
and Tennessee) beaded

up like a red plastic stud
against your collar

or if not there, strange wet
lady at checkout express,

then on your sleeve
or even the hem

of your hopelessly
ugly, sexy, very

corduroy pants.

Bow Hunting in Nevada

In Heaven, in the sagebrush, will there be sparrow hawks to eat the sparrows, and if so, what will eat them or will everybody eat melon and honey and then get ready to sing. Do ants and flies have their own Heaven? Do Catholics? Can we shoot guns in Heaven, maybe something nice, engraved and with inlay. Who will do the inlaying and from whom will we get the ivory, the silver, the walnut stock. What if Heaven only has softwoods, junk trees, crook grain and pith. It doesn't have to be guns. What if the deer in their perfected and restored bodies can run so far and so fast no 150-grain carbon fiber shaft two-inch vane arrow can leave my bow and ever catch up? More singing I guess. How long can you sing—days, weeks? Can we go to hell and torment the wretches? They are dead and in hell already, so what could be worse?

Not any visit by us, surely.

All Males Die after Mating

Quolls live in Australia and don't blame me, I didn't design them. I am just here to tell you the things that may be on the GRE. Or else maybe God is a woman—because here it is, between thylacine and numbat, *A Field Guide to Mammals of Australia*, second edition, page 48, the northern quoll: "all males die after mating." Mermaids too, and most species of butterfly. You have to admit, it's almost worth it. Whenever I have been spending an hour or two mating, I cannot eat lunch afterward because I have to spin in a circle until I throw up, just to make room inside for the extra feelings. Perhaps it is the same for you, which explains the roller skate key you keep in your glove box, next to the roll of quarters and the sunglasses with star-shaped lenses. Some day I want to have made love in every state in America, and to have stood on the car afterward, waving flags and shooting guns.

Until then we will eat a picnic lunch at this roadside rest. How much longer until Colorado? Nebraska seems to be lasting so much longer than Iowa, and most animals seem to live such shorter, happier lives than we do.

Landscape Is Just

Highly pigmented powder. Applies evenly, blends well. And
the eye pencils in this set stay sharp, glide easily, providing

a brownish- or reddish-gray, slope-forming, unsorted mixture

subtle, flirty, or sultry eyes that stay in place all day. An array
of hues and finishes, from matte to glimmer—

of mud, silt, sand, pebbles, cobbles, and boulders. Clasts angular

in shades for everyone. The lip glosses are beautiful,
substantive, and long wearing. Go from demure

to rounded and locally consilidated by calcite and gypsum. Zero

to all-out-wow in minutes; only your imagination limits the looks
you can create. These waterproof eye shadows come this year

hour sandstone, limestone, and chert clasts in gravelly matrix

in a stunning array. Limited time only. Colors in this set

occupy low gradient, low energy drainages. Entire substrate
subject to sheet wash,

extensive at times,

subject to getting drunk in bars, meeting somebody,
biting right through the back

of his blue denim shirt.

This Is Not an Ekphrastic Poem

but never mind that now, and instead, in appreciation of Rousseau, *Scouts Attacked by a Tiger*, I just need to say that from here on out, obviously all tigers should be shaped like accordions, and what about the dead scout, floral in a yellow muumuu and floating on blades of grass as tall as Rousseau on Sunday horseback, the dead scout dreaming of violins

even as Le Douanier paints and paints, singing. Stage left, the moon-sun hides the daylight inside the butter. Scout 2 rides his horse like dirty laundry, laundry that rides a horse that doubles as a stingray. Even the gilded frame writhes, bouquet of fingertips. Still, never mind the frame, it's that tiger—we must do something. Shouldn't we do something? I would sell my children

to paint like this—no, that's not true. I would sell my children and some of yours too to be the kind of man who could sell his children for smears of paint. Welcome to the new France: even the iron scrollwork applauds. White pullets in the coop, dirigible-bodied children swollen under hot air balloons, sashes with medals: good morning, 1904. It makes me

want to paint my lawn again and again until (like Rousseau's) it can comb its hair with daylight. No, I want to break into the frame and steal the air trapped inside wads of paint, Rousseau's breath pressed into the pigment like black ants in red amber. Lick the painting and you lick his hands, his face. Drill a hole in the frame and blow out the yolk,

save the meaning in a perfect oology of genius. Rousseau does not need us; the scouts though do; they are Hindu or probably Muslim, and there is nobody on hand to wash their bodies, say the right prayers, lay them out in honor. Every painting implies a *what's next*, and we need to hurry up, the tiger is slaughtering these poor men.

Maybe we could tranquilize the beast, relocate it to some meadow of fruit trees and masochistic deer, deer that maybe were all war criminals once, so they deserve to die. Maybe the tiger is a Buddhist, wants to be vegetarian, just give it a chance. Maybe it will get bored, fall asleep. Maybe tigers are afraid of masks. Put this on. What would Picasso do?

Maybe I will hide in a toilet stall in the men's room: after closing, when the guard kills the lights, I will still be there waiting, just me and Picasso and a few hired guns, all waiting to lock and load and climb inside the picture and when I give the signal, ready to rush to help repopulate the sad and desperate world

of *Scouts Attacked by a Tiger*, oil on canvas, Barnes Foundation, Philadelphia, USA.

The Life of Jasper Johns

As a child, he moved often. That explains so little maybe

A longtime assistant to Jasper Johns pleaded guilty on Wednesday

it explains everything. Count stars in any potential original:

after selling 22 artworks he stole from the artist's Connecticut studio.

50 mean it is a fake since back then flags had 48. He said

(The record price for a work by Mr. Johns, set at Christie's in 2010?

"Thank goodness art still tends to be less what critics write

$28.6 million.) In January, a Queens foundry owner pleaded guilty

than what artists make." He did like the idea of periscopes

after selling fraudulent bronze made from one of Mr. Johns's molds.

pushing up through a gallery floor, having a look around.

The assistant created false registration certificates, even fake pages

Most of Johns's sculptures are based on the everyday trash

from a three-ring binder in which Johns writes inventory numbers.

he has in his studio—a light bulb, a coffee can of turpentine

He only made $4 million, has to give it back, will go to jail for years

blossoming with a bouquet of paint brushes. Many days

and years. Indictment led to a plea deal: interstate transportation

even he does not know what is serious, what is a joke.

of stolen property, which carries a rather hefty maximum sentence.

He seems not to care. He is just glad not to be moving

The assistant expresses regret for his actions and his betrayal of trust.

a lot. He is glad when people mostly just leave him alone.

Sargent Never Painted

my wife or her family,
davenport royalty

who spend hours
explaining

To prepare peaches for canning,
first you must scold them.

Over Tastykakes
and Penn Dark

we try to decide: is it
crayfish or crawdad?

Answer to the question,
why are there so many states,

because when you get to one
that doesn't sell beer on Sundays,

it's always good to know
how quickly and easily

you can drive someplace else.

You're Like This Girl in Lone Pine

She said she wasn't wearing any underwear,
needed a ride.

She said, *Call me Coney Island*. She could
pee standing up. She said we should

find a crater, write our names in the snow
with urine. She used another word,

Russian slang, but I knew what she meant.
It was crazy, but haven't you looked out like that,

said to yourself, what's just past the edge that I can't see,
and past that part too, what's past that?

I think you have. You are shattered by distance
daily, know too that starlight is just scar tissue

shining through the powder burns.
When I reach out to touch your face

my hand goes all the way through.

Pelt Vault, Natural History Museum

Okapi, elk, jackal, tiger:
behind trophy-head bear

skulls and the mothballed
rows of birds in drawers,

deep inside the Pelt Vault
the hides drape over rods

like tiers of scalped brides.
I want to unzip my face,

join them, but my poetry friend
just wants to date all of them,

give them each a private day
at the prom with flowers.

Art friend draws like crazy;
it's mane and stripe Surplus Mart,

a perfect ocean of inside
out. Soft as water, ocelot

1550 was found already
dead, hit by a car, Brazil,

but eland 2289 was taken
with a Texas heart shot—

what it is called to shoot
an animal from behind,

through the anus,
killing it more or less

swiftly but mostly
keeping the hide

perfectly
intact.

Somewhere Near the Rental Car Counter

Ill luck beset Grayson: he was shipwrecked; his son was murdered;
he went bankrupt; he died of yellow fever. A dove, a mockingbird,

and a mammal are named after him. Heermann's gull, as in
a man who surveyed for the railroads, coined the word *oology*,

died shot by his own rifle. Due to syphilis, Heermann looked older
than his own father. The Russians exiled Stegmann to Kazakhstan.

To pass time, he studied muskrats. Xavier of the Congo wrote
an article about an earthquake; shortly after, the Petrified Forest

was described by Woodhouse. Charles Wright was unpopular after
Japan, was asked to leave the ship in San Francisco. Prof. Woodward

drowned; his twin brother did not. Wombey in Australia discovered
the most venomous snake in the world. Forskål—killed by plague,

Yemen. Mary Ann Hume, wife of Allan Hume, a poet. Umberto
Raineri Carlo Emanuele Giovanni Maria Ferdinando Eugenio of Savoy,

king of Italy and finder of Humbert's Cardinal, was assassinated
in 1900 by Gaetano Basso. Haynaldi, Hungarian botanist, otherwise

unknown. Emin Pasha's real name was Isaak Schnitzer. Even lovers
did not know. Janos Xantus de Vesey collected 10,000 specimens

and was a pathological liar. Ludwig Lorenz, 1904, finder of the only known
specimen of Lorenz's Seedeater, forged the record—bird never existed;

he made it from parts. Van Wyck drowned in a typhoon; his son died
at the Little Bighorn. Vassal died in the Congo. Grant, intelligence officer

in Abyssinia, searched for the Nile but did not find the headwaters;
Speke did. Rolf Grantsau, Brazil, went twice to Antarctica. A beetle

and carnivorous plant are named for him. I have been to Antarctica
as well, twice in fact, yet nobody has named anything for me or at least

not yet. I have been to Easter Island and to a dodgy restaurant in Shanghai
owned by the mafia. My wife is not a countess; she has no hummingbirds

named for her. Our dictionary entries will be blank, or perhaps will say,
He drove an old car, rarely got tickets. An out-of-print book on leprosy ranks

higher than me on Amazon. I have seen the Nile; it was mostly brown,
smoggy. My kids are okay, not movie stars. My wife is slow, forgetful,

often needy—no, that is my dog. In New Guinea I watched swiftlets
fly through spider webs and trail glistening strands of iridescence

as they banked from shadow to sun to shadow. It was pretty good.
I would do that again if I could. So far nobody has named a beetle,

not even a fly after me, because of it. Maybe next time. Maybe soon.
I sure hope so.

Street Trees of San Francisco

Monkey-puzzle, a nice tree, native to the South Pacific. Bark peels off in slim curls, like the shavings from a black sunburn.

Camphor, related to cinnamon. Plant this if you enjoy replacing your sidewalk.

Pepper trees, bored as teenagers. Meyer lemons, from China, doing well. To add flavor to a risotto made with mascarpone and Parmesan, add grated Meyer peel. Makes the kitchen smell grandmother nice plus prevents scurvy.

Bristlecone pine. Inside, the grain is a kind of skin clock—here is when you were born. Here is the Jayhawk War, and this, by it, that is the circle when Henry Thoreau was alive, sending turtles in alcohol to Spencer Baird at the Smithsonian. Here is a fifty-year drought. Here is a hundred-year one. This cluster marks the Avignon Papacy; hippos by now have started to become rare in Egypt. This part is Jesus, when lions still occurred in Sicily. Tigers came to Rome from Asia Minor, not far. Elephants were everywhere. Somebody you're related to was alive then, your fingerprints quoting theirs like love letters from your parents' parents' parents. Taste the sap, smoky brandy.

This tree looks like your elbows—here, take a picture.

This tree has narrow slits like windows so the bats can look out, see if it is nighttime yet, and if you knock on the trunk sometimes a small monkey will stick its head out. *Once upon a time there was a child just like you.* How much of my life has been spent listening for the end to that story? If I wait in this coffee shop long enough, dinner will finally come. Then the moon will rise above jacarandas and the streets will dissolve like my childhood, which had a lot of ashtrays and strange, tall people who tugged at their knees before sitting down. How easy it is to imagine being a kind of sultan or absolute sun king, strict but fair—strict but fair and handsome as a whip, the kind of king also just wise enough to know that justice should be popular, which is why prisoners will need to be executed in public and why every street in my kingdom will be lined with rows and rows of tall and useful trees.

On the Island of the Not-So-Broken Poets

I know names of horses—Roy Rogers's, Dale Evans's, Tom Mix's (it was Tony)—and 200 kinds of animals without needing a book. Could be worse: what if you were married to me? Kate Gale said to me at a reading in Santa Monica on a day so blue it made postcards hurt, "When you come down to it" (after I corrected Eloise Klein Healy about the taxonomy of North American bears), "facts are overrated." I think she meant men, that men are overrated, and guns too, and the penis more generally. What can I say? She's right, but even so, it is the grizzly bear that's on the California flag, and it's the kind that is extirpated, not the black bear, and the white spirit bears of coastal British Colombia are the black bear kind, not the grizzly bear kind, and neither is at all related to the polar bear kind, even though global warming causes interbreeding in isolated cases. Vaduz—capital of Liechtenstein, it might come up some day, you never know. And hey, Eloise? Hi, it's me, and just so you know, about the bears, I am sorry, and if there were a muddy part of the road and you needed to cross, I would lay down my coat for you while I am still inside of it, and I would wait for you even if you wanted to go back and forth ten or twenty times.

Ikea

Okay pal, the dog said to me. Enough is enough. We had a deal. My turn now. Hey, I said, don't scratch the headboard, it's expensive. We just got that.

Now I live in the yard. I don't remember any deal.

Funeral Plans

When I realize I'll die first, before my kids
or even my exes,

I wonder about the funeral—

who will sit with whom,
who will dress up nice,

and when I tell that to my wife,
she says, *Get real—*

you think I am inviting any of those bitches?

The Dictionary of Artists' Models

If painting is female and insanity is a female malady, then all women painters are mad and all male painters are women.

—MARLENE DUMAS

Nothing is known about **A** before or after her years with Matisse.

B did crossword puzzles while working.

Oskar Kokoschka never got over **C**; he had a full-size mannequin constructed in her likeness. He would cut off its head at parties.

D appears in 384 paintings by Bonnard. When she died, he closed the door to her bedroom and never entered it again.

Klimt's **E** was allergic to cats and had a clear, loud sneeze.

Krohg met **F** at the Jockey Club and begged her to let him paint her; his wife was dating Pascin, who committed suicide. Later F sold books from a stall on the Seine.

Toulouse-Lautrec called **G** La Mélinite, "anarchists' dynamite."

Man Ray made a deck of cards; **H** was the Queen of Clubs and had two faces.

I is buried in Igdlorssuit, Greenland, in an unnumbered grave.

No portraits of **J** survive. According to neighbors, she died of a drug overdose, alone in a hotel, during the war, in Paris.

Turner had two children by **K**. In his will he left the children money but revoked hers. Turner and his father shared a house until the father died at age 84; neighbors believed the children may have been the father's, not Turner's.

L is best known for being the Weeping Woman of *Guernica*. The more Picasso distorted her face, the more L said it was all right because he was not Picasso painting L, he was Picasso painting a Picasso.

M was Cellini's mistress, dates unknown, as were **N** and **O**, dates also unknown. He said he liked to have sex with the Holy Trinity before starting work.

Stanley Spencer wrote hundred-page letters to **P**, even after she died. He said he always loved her, even during the five years he left her to live with his other model, **Q**. In one resurrection scene, he included P's body three times.

Tsuguharu Foujita tattooed a siren on **R**'s thigh. He left his wife for her and later married her but then left her for **S**, fleeing with the new model to Brazil.

In Africa, **T** washed Peter Beard's face when he had malaria, shot two snakes with a revolver, let him rub her with the entrails of just-killed zebras. Interviewed about that time, she only would say, *A sharp knife is less likely to cut you than a dull one.*

U hangs in the Met; she always thought Degas was a humbug.

When **V** showed up to work, the instructor complained, "They told me you would be more Rubenesque." "No," she told him, "Even better. Tonight you get Courbet."

W is known to biographers only by finger quotes, as "W."

X was active in the Resistance; caught, she was being transferred to Ravensbrück when U.S. planes strafed her train and she escaped. She died in Paris of old age.

Y told her family she quit art to become a knife thrower's model in the circus. It was easier than telling them she had married into royalty and no, she wouldn't give them any money.

When **Z** met Picasso she was 21 and already had degrees from the Sorbonne and Cambridge, had started law school and dropped out, was making a living as an artist despite the Nazi occupation of Paris. Early work destroyed by bombs. Appeared in *Life* magazine. After ten years, tired of Picasso, left him, wrote a book about him and against his opposition, won the right to publish it. It sold a million copies. Later edited *Virginia Woolf Quarterly*, designed stage sets for the Guggenheim, taught at USC, married Jonas Salk. Asked if it was true, that Picasso wanted to see her before he died, Z would only say that Picasso wanted to see a lot of things, including the face of God, and she hoped when it happened both of them would be ready.

Magazine Tiger, *Harper's Bazaar*

Thorstein Veblen, *Theory of the Leisure Class*, 1899,
such as this lady in salt linen on a seamless backdrop

bottle-feeding a baby white tiger. (Bottle, $5.95.
Jacket, $1,980.) Listen as even her earlobes explain

how to look good in heels. I feel naked. Somebody
has made the tiger wear a diamond collar. (Collar,

$3,935. Lipstick, $39.) Somebody else had to clean
the tiger's pen, twice. All in all, it's going well.

The tiger is hot under the lights but the producers
have insurance, sedatives, extra bowls of water.

The tiger is so clean its fur could be a boutique hotel.
In the ad our hopes are named *fetlock, femur, intestine,*

shoulder blade. The image is smart, confident, and slim,
tells us that only humans should be the most terrible

of the animals. By now the gaffers and half the handlers
would lick the model's shoes for her number but it's a wrap,

that went well, thank you everybody. The tiger waits
to be loaded into the back of a truck. The model

waits on page 82. The world waits patiently before
crushing us into powder with the immense weight

of its beauty and indifference.

The History of Hell in America

*And I guess you can get to Limbo
the same way you got here:
by mistake.*

—PAUL VIOLI, "LITTLE TESTAMENT"

The History of Hell in America

In the beginning hell was cool, nearly cold.
Hell had horses and blown-ash handprints—
Hades in manganese, we say now, trying to parse
the terse semiotics of the Upper Paleolithic.
Feel the clay: that hell was narrow, wet,
lit only by cupped bowls of fat and moths
of frosted breath, the beneath that is beneath
beneath. Then glaciers melted into green rivers
of grass and the wind turned the voices of larks
into running children. Feral anise, bricks and roads,
tawny bundles of wheat: for the Sumerians,
hell was a word pressed into clay, something
named, written down. *Ganz'r*, it was called;
as in Egypt's hell, one could eat millet there,
watch birds, own slaves and boats, celebrate
the inventory of one's umbrellas and plows.
There was such a thing as sin, and sin, like
sand or lice, had weight, the heft of the soul
balanced against weight of an endured life.
Strife and dualism followed: top and bottom,
wrong and right—Zoroastrian hell pushed back
against Zoroastrian heaven, the singing place.
Temperatures walked higher with each telling:
hell was a set of boxes. Would you rather be alone
for all of eternity or packed tight as fish in urns?
Misery needs company, thought the Greeks,
so they named the rivers that: Styx ("hatred"),
and its tributaries—Woe, Burning, Wailing,
and *Lethe*, to forget. The Greek dead needed
blood but rarely got it. There is reincarnation,
Plato's Socrates claimed, and souls in judgment
flare like light from the windows of a granary
just as winter's stores are touched by the rushes
of the barbarians. What is most dear to us burns
brightest. In Greek hell most sinners received fire
and scourge, but the philosophers explained how

philosophers were welcomed into the company
of the gods. Even so, think as you would act,
because an instrument of torment is but a failed
copy of the idea of an instrument of torment,
and one day you may both attain a final purity
of form, matched by an equal purity of justice.
She'ol, Jewish hell, can be translated Pit, Grave,
Garbage Heap. Its unclean dead were little more
than the rags burned after burying plague victims.
Strange ice: in this hell, heavy scabs glowed,
wide clouds changing shape as they cooled,
metal hissing with the hot summer rain.
Were there seven heavens, or ten? Answers
flew away like angry crows, and who knew
or cared where slaves went when they died.
In good years, the afterbirth of golden ewes
covered the graves of the patriarchs; even the
servants had enough bread. Like a sprung lid
hell could open suddenly; after the Crucifixion
Christ harrowed hell, the freed souls spiraling up
like a funnel cloud of pink-faced, white-hot bats.
Better not to spend too long with such visions—
the simple act of gliding plane along the clean grain,
cedar trued by level and square, can prove answers
to last a lifetime. Poachers' snares, the thief's garrote:
history squeezed the throat of the Roman Empire
while Gnostics and Manichaeans argued that the world
is hell: we live in it already, just take a look around.
Still, papyrus grew and was cut, the rains came,
ibis beaks probed flooded fields of fallow rice.
According to scribes, what does not change
is the will to change, so hell came to Africa
early, carried up the Nile by barge and dhow,
faith following shipments of slaves, resin, pigs,
salt. Hell reached Ethiopia by 300, a mix of
Hebraic vengeance, Alexandrine theology,
and Coptic asceticism. It felt new as fire
and the Bishop of Nubia called theirs true
Christianity, but it did not last; Islam spread
like a tent, killing in shadow all it did
not convert. By 900, Timbuktu's hell

was *Gehenna*, seven-chambered Moslem
hades, and gazelles grazing among thorns
cocked their ears, watched the caravans
pass, honor guards armed with tall rifles
embossed with ivory and brass. Love
implies matching hate, and hell's light lights
more than one breakaway sect's nave,
the stained glass of each apostate site
glowing with inverted sunrise. Go forth
and spread the news: Christ is arisen
and his tomb shall be our sanctuary.
This is the magma of his breath, Pyrex
chalice brimming with the scalding acid
of his blood. This is a lock of his hair—
smell it as it burns. How much pain
would you be willing to assume to replace
the pain of another? To know when to keep
the Sabbath the father should take an empty
bottle, fill it each week with seven stones.
On the first day, at sundown, remove
one stone, and when the last stone lifts out,
call the family and servants to the compound
and say, "This is the day the Prophet said
to worship God. Go and wash yourselves,
and become clean for prayer." *The Levant*,
it said on maps: Jerusalem was a kind of hell
for some, an intense, almost sexual release
of martyrdom for others. The pope in Avignon
could feel it coming, felt ill at ease, restless,
could not sleep. In Rome, candles plumed tall
then went out; a strange wind blew. Rivers
smelled like blood; all who saw it agreed a calf
had been born with two heads. Even stars broke
into pieces with the urgency of the warnings.
Reform, *reform*, whispered each falling light,
reform the church or lose it. Milton's Satan spoke
better English than Shakespeare because
he had to: Jesuits walked hundreds of miles
resurrecting Bosch and Dante. Incandescent
with fever, Valignano brought hell to Japan,
de Nobili to India, Father Ricci to China.

With a lamp and a smile, Pedro Páez learned
eleven languages in order to reconvert Ethiopia.
"Yes," he explained, "there is a separate purgatory
of lesser fire for unbaptized babies who die at birth;
our God is a fair God, a just God." How many devils
are there in hell? 133,306,668—as computed by
Alphonsus de Spina, a good man, and Catholic.
One demon is called Andras; he has a naked body
and an owl's head. Abduscius uproots trees;
the devil called Bune has three heads and moves
bodies from one grave to another. To create
a lasting religion one needs frame and narrative
as in all art, which may be why when they killed
Father Páez, S.J., they pulled out his tongue
and saved it in a jar. In the Enlightenment
hell was located in the center of the sun, proven
by calm science to be the only place hot enough;
by the time of Keats, for most sweeps, rag pickers,
or inhabitants of Bedlam, hell was just London.
John Wesley was buried in the same churchyard
as William Blake, yews old and tall on all sides.
In most parts of Southern Africa, Methodists
could be told by their plows, and because unlike dogs,
they had two names. To avoid hell, plant a garden
and wear shoes. On Sunday, have lamb with mint,
Mother's old recipe. Regular meals, regular hours,
regular days: let life imitate the order of heaven
and there will be less shock in the transference
when it is time to go. Hell followed the salt cod
and Basque whalers to America early, left a while,
came back, left, then like smallpox and snuff boxes,
stayed for good. John James Audubon praised
the yellows and reds of the Carolina Parakeet,
shot twenty-five. To the young woman taken away
by Indians and treated well, taught to chew hide
or knap flint, her life was different but the same,
sometimes even better. Her family's torment
was not hers, and, being rescued and returned,
theirs became hers again. Whose pain is worse:
the child abducted; that of the parents; or priest
or lay pastor when he realizes how the full plan

of abduction and loss is just as God intended?
Here are some Choctaw, thin and hungry;
let's kill them. The ground is too hard to dig
for graves, too hard for potatoes or corn;
once spring thaws the soil, bury them then
or just let the dogs enact the justice of God.
The world here mirrors the world there,
yet do ravens eat the testicles of the dead
in heaven, or are they without appetite, perhaps
not present at all? Perhaps only in hell do children
eat from dumpsters, or cry alone, their underwear
soiled by the semen of monsters. The Shakers
believed one could start in hell but evolve onward,
since soul's probation is not limited to this world
but extends to the world of spirits, future state.
God was equal parts female and male, forgiveness
and exact justice. To be ecstatic was to be alive
to the presence of both heaven and hell, and in
junior high, in church camp, I sang and sang,
a candle of feeling whose wick started in my feet
and ran into my head like a bundle of loud cloth.
In the deep South, some days hell would last
from morning until dark: because he was white,
my father made 40 cents a day picking tobacco;
blacks were just given 25. Said John Wesley,
"If no Devil, then no God." (And Nietzsche,
"Even God has His hell: it is His love for Man.")
To be American is to be eccentric, preaching
to 30,000 like Aimee Semple McPherson
or else building vast networks of railroads
in your basement, hoarding cans of beans
or Eisenhower dollars. Raise your hand
if you want to be saved. Desert pioneer
John Samuelson could not abide the smell
of other humans, and in the 1920s, just as rain
patterns changed and the Mojave no longer
supported cattle, he homesteaded 300 acres
out past the village of Joshua Tree, where
Gram Parsons died and the park is now.
His windmill vane's logo said, AERMOTOR,
CHICAGO. Heaven was a good well's driveshaft,

lubricating oil kept ready in a spout-topped can,
bushings milled by Bessemer. He wrote poetry,
smoked hand-rolleds. With a tin of lard and
a skillet, you can do okay. Fifty-pound sack
of cornmeal costs 4 dollars, lasts weeks.
Far away in another state somebody else had
picked it, shucked it, ground it, packed it.
Were they paid enough even to buy dinner?
Not his problem, the problems of others,
he said, nailing siding. He had a hammer,
a chisel, and a set of beliefs he needed
to say out loud. GOD MADE MAN, he carved
directly into the blue patina of the granite,
BUT HENRY FORD PUT WHEELS UNDER 'EM.
Desert varnish it's called, good for petroglyphs
and madmen—chip away dark veneer so
paler rock glows underneath, ready page,
lit slate, crank's billboard. On boulders
big as houses he carved hard thoughts,
journals six feet tall and wide as swan wings.
What cancer art burns your mouth so badly
you would cut your language directly into
raw stone? Samuelson's Rocks it's called,
out near Twentynine Palms, *semper fidelis*,
largest Marine base in the world. Jets mock-
strafe hikers and bighorn, because they can,
because young men always will be young
and infinite. The jet exhaust smells
like lighter fluid and spent matches.
It is a better place to be black, though,
the Marines, than most other barrios, because
nation-states need the poor and their armies:
Samuelson died the year Mussolini invaded
Ethiopia, tanks passing rock-cut churches,
the same year Stalin destroyed half of his
own churches, history purged clean of hell
even as he created it. Thomas Thompson
ministered to blacks in the Carolinas and,
later, West Africa. In 1769 as a vicar
in Kent he wrote his memoir, titled
The African Trade for Negro Slaves, Shewn

to be Consistent with the Principles of Humanity
and with the Laws of Revealed Religion.
How should his descendants apologize,
and what would you say, if you met one?
I remember a sign in Florida, HELL IS TRUTH
SEEN TOO LATE. Felt hat cocked, chisel
striking sparks, John Samuelson wrote

> RELIGION IS A CODE OF
> MORALLS FOR US TO LIVE BY
> NO MORE. HELL IS HERE ON THIS
> EARTH NO OTHER PLASE.
> MOST OF IT WE MAKE OUR SELF
> AS TO HAVEN FIND IT IN
> A LIFETIME NOTHING
> PROVEN AFTER DEATH BY PREAST
> OR SCIENTIST.

You can spell heaven *haven* or you can spell it
Abyssinia, invading it with tanks or on foot,
staff in hand, peregrine pilgrim. Either way
you bring the dome of your skull with you,
canopy of sky you cannot escape, as black
or white as your dreams allow. C. S. Lewis:
"The Lord finds our desires not too strong,
but too weak." After shooting Kennedy,
Lee Harvey Oswald went to the movies;
Cry Battle came on first and *War Is Hell*
was the double feature. There was the smell
of aftershave, butter in the lobby's clear-boxed
machinery. It was dim, reassuringly so,
and I see him smoking in the dark, hands
shielding Zippo as he lights a new one,
and the screen, for a moment, loses
focus behind a silvery veil of smoke.
"At the ends of things, the Blessed will say,
'We have never lived anywhere except in Heaven,'
and the Lost, 'We were always in Hell.'
And both will speak truly."

Escape Velocity

Above me I saw something I did not believe at first. Well above the haze layer of the earth's atmosphere were additional faint thin bands of blue, sharply etched against the dark sky. They hovered over the earth like a succession of halos.

—DAVID SIMONS, FIRST BALLOON RIDE ABOVE 100,000 FEET, 1957

Sunrise on Mercury

A woman in a bar once told me I looked like matches

waiting for an arsonist. A man said, *If you could lick my heart,*
it would poison you. That is why I often wear a thick shirt

and sturdy gloves. All her life my daughter was a comet—

no, first she was a cat with grease pencil whiskers and black tights.
Halloween had fallen on a weekend: my father had shown up too,

his heart already leaky as a Russian freighter. Trick or treat,

except we had to wait a bit while my dad sat on a low wall
and explained to us all how he didn't need to sit on a wall.

I have decided I'll tell the doctor that, and how ice runs

in the family, but I will tell him it's a kind of moon ice,
asphalt bands of smalt and grit. Welcome to the scenario

called how to be a man waiting on a very hard chair

in the lobby of rehab. I am a man who washes his own car,
or at least who says he does. I know how to spackle things

cleanly and well. When driving, I pretend I am flying a jet

that fires rockets. Real men should change their own oil,
be able to sleep through the television in waiting rooms.

Go ahead, shoot me with a ray beam. It will bounce off.

Time now to pretend that I am the kind of dad who gets
up smartly and shakes hands even as the doctor tells me

my daughter has been moved to a new ward, now can have

shoelaces. Hand out. Both feet wide. *Pleased to meet you.*
A few Halloweens later when Amber was maybe fifteen

she became a vampire bride, blood and ice-white lace

in thrift store wedding dress. Was she drinking, even then?
The rest of us twist the burn slowly, hoping that the meat

of the body lasts a long time. My father points—*See that oil?*

You need a ring job. If we all lived on Mercury, this is what
we would see: the sun would rise, stall, go backward a few days,

set, rise, and finally hurry the rest of the way across.

It would be huge: be sure to wear your special glasses.
The first photograph of Mercury was taken in 1838;

I am in it. My father used to get mad when I said things

like that. He got mad in the garage when repairs broke
again. Real men know how to sleep through a bus ride

or a lecture by their fathers. Are you lazy or just stupid?

Trick question: both, Dad, both. He went to church
more often than I do, was a good man more times

a day than I ever am. Some days I still want to pee

two feet farther than him, mostly to say I've done it.
That phrase in French, *l'heure bleue*: nautical twilight

overlapping with astronomical twilight, both not full

dark and yet no longer daylight. Not so unhappy
yet not happy either: welcome to *la vie quotidienne.*

Sometimes a dim, diluted music fills me like milk

in a painting by Vermeer. More things to make me
just like my father. At night, when trucks pass, dogs

pull to the ends of their chains and yell his name.

Sometimes I join in. See how well my tools hang
large to small from their pegs. Look at my clean car.

Compared to my father, I am better organized, better

at getting even. I prop my children upright in blue fish
tank sand like the glow sticks that they are. Grown-up

teeth fill my mouth in well-marked rows. I have a wallet,

a haircut punch card. Two more then free. My father
once saw a hand cut off, in the war. Fury in the telling

would rise in him like black sap. My own wounds

I have learned to tap with a little metal spigot.
We each hunch over, tending our gardens, afraid

somebody will see. When I die, like a Mormon

I will give all my children their own planets.
Here, you can have Mercury. When I die,

I promise not to come back.

Getting Home without Tom Hanks

In the movie *Apollo 13* when the oxygen tanks explode on the way to Venus the crew needs some kind of gravitational boost to get home. Not too big, not too small. They need to pivot back around the right way, using some moon or minor planet as a belay for the come-around. If only Venus still had a moon, but it doesn't—hasn't for ten million years, as the whiz kid explains to the waitress. It is Tom Hanks who thinks up a way to make a time machine out of spare parts. They will go back to the moment when a red-hot moon fell out of orbit and crashed into the magma that was back-in-the-day Venus, go back and capture that surplus energy to slingshot home, then once on the way, hyper-jump back into the right time stream. They all agree—tricky, but it just *might* work. Later it is the whiz kid again who, at the moment when all they need is just one more piece of wire, thinks to use the underwire from the waitress's bra and who, in a sweet scene, promises not to look as she takes off her clothes down to her panties. The camera watches, but—shy and loyal—the kid does not. Who will die, we still wonder, thinking it will have to be the PE coach, especially since he's black and in the flashback scene was the one who gave the team spirit pep talk to the football squad at halftime. But no, it turns out it is Tom Hanks himself who will have to die on the way back, and we realize why: he is the one who defiled the temple by watching as the waitress undressed, watched like an elder at the well and so polluted them all with his unclean actions. It is his finest moment in the movie when he kisses her and herds them into the lander and bolts the hatch shut, then stays behind in the vast parental loneliness of space, waving a wry good-bye through the cold glass forever.

The Earth as Seen from Earth

1.

People used to be three feet tall. They stood by lightning
strikes, tasting the charcoal from burned trees, moonlight

silvering their fur. Before that we were proto-simians
like bush babies, like the ones in Sri Lanka called loris

that I have looked for on two trips and still not seen.
We used to be eaten by owls, leopards, other people,

leaving us afraid of snakes and anything hinky like rain
or odd noises, like whatever makes a mom wake up,

reach for a 9mm, blow the brains out of the man by the bed
who turns out to be her middle son, come home so late

because somebody stole his car, he had to walk from Sixth
and Broadway, five miles, he just wanted to tell her not

to worry, they stole his phone too, but he's home now.

2.

My, what ugly feet they had, they will think in 100 years
when salvage crews on the Sea of Tranquility plaster

cast our footprints. Back then my father had dopey ears
like LBJ. In the 1960s you could usually leave your keys

in the car, it would be okay. I knew grown-ups named
Butch and Dutch. It was Sunday, cooling marine layer,

dew point 61 degrees, July 1969, the astronauts waiting
for me inside the house, but I was behind cinderblock

saying *Mister, please*. Nixon wasn't yet a fallen angel. Janis
Joplin was still alive, doing 200 dollars a day of smack.

Gasoline was free. Back then walking was still a normal
way to get around: I used to cut behind the SP tracks,

back when we all were happy just to be lit up by the sky
all day and night. I remember 1969 and the one before,

1968, the Tet Offensive, I remember when writing
on my Keds in math class in pen was a kind of high

thin plane of perfection. We wore white ovals on
our shirts with words in red italics. I remember

when Jesus had blue eyes in the storybooks
in Sunday school—we had such fast cars then,

and at the zoo, when I saw a kind of bush baby
called a galago, I remember telling my brother

that was him a week after he was born. I remember
when we didn't use paper money at all: instead,

we just bought and sold things with cruelty.

3.

My best friend used to say, "Let's go to the dump,
shoot the rats," even though we lived in the desert

so there was no dump. He just meant, go out,
make something happen. Or shoot dogs:

another thing to do at a dump. Somebody
always has a bead on somebody else. Shills

watch the marks getting off the bus in Santa
Monica, or in the tropics you can watch snakes

waiting to eat the bats as they leave the cave.
Even if you can fly in the dark, something waits

to touch you. What happened to the astronauts
who trained for but never got to go to the moon?

Did they feel a vague, numb loss, the way one
for years later can still sense a phantom limb?

And whatever happened to the 2 a.m. woman
who killed her son? She shot herself a year later.

Never mind the history of who had stood there
by her bed before that time, what else happened.

What have you done you can't talk about out loud?
She couldn't eat, she lost weight, she tried it all—

cutting off her hair, working in soup kitchens,
sewing the eyelids back onto the faces of children

killed in bomb blasts in Tel Aviv—nothing,
nada. To take her turn she used a gun again.

Usually it is pills. We are trained to die lined up
by gender. Unlike Amundsen or Robert Falcon

Scott, the members of the 1912 Japanese Antarctic
expedition were good Buddhists, ate miso pickles

and polished rice, could not eat or shoot their dogs,
so after the ice shelf broke, they had to sail away

leaving the dogs behind, one group shouting
and pounding on the deck of the moving ship,

the other group racing back and forth on the shore,
the language between them older than snow, each

of them wondering, *How could we have let this happen*.

4.

We did not land on the moon, we landed in Mojave,
Las Vegas, Pittsburgh. We landed on television:

feet walking around inside each set. Not conspiracy,
that's just how reality works. Look up: even a drunk

can still find the moon. Maybe a few miles away?
Smaller than aspirin. How many is a million miles.

More than people in line at the post office. After
that, math becomes meaningless, like love letters

from Japanese explorers written right to left, like
weather reports from foreign countries. If God

let the moon happen, why not two or three more?
In time they would become familiar, just there.

Rounding third, somebody has just won the World
Series. Try to remember the slant of the front teeth

in his smile, the way the dirt powders his knees
like an ad for soap, the exact *thwack* of the moon-

white ball when it clears the fence, drifting casually,
bored by gravity. The grass must be full of old

moons, broken stars, bottle caps, used-up bat handles.
We did not land on the moon: it never happened,

which is pretty good, since when we give back 1969,
that means we can give back the death of Hendrix,

the first twenty years of the Cold War, the beginning
of the end of gasoline. We keep the desert sky clean

just for ourselves. We never landed on the moon;
the sleeping woman never shot her son; in Antarctica,

the dogs found connecting floes, jumped back on ship.
In 1969 nobody ever had touched my face, my penis;

I only wore white cowboy shirts to school, because
that was what I wanted. My father left most days

in the dark. When he stood by the car, smoking,
the moon sometimes was nearly round, nearly

perfect as the buttons on my best new shirt.

Mars with Fear and Dread:

1. Phobos

This one looks bent, not a moon
and this one also says *I'm sorry*

sky's late-for-work dry peach
its own bunched shadow, sets

a day. Ugly as sin. A moon
by the U.S. Naval Observatory,

means something important
just that part in the *Iliad*

when Ares in school Latin
twins Dread and Fear. Do we

care? In 1877 even the sky
astronomy. He had married

who found this moon. 1877:
and a Vanderbilt; Crazy Horse

bayonetted from behind. This was
or take. You were fear and dread,

A white corset sleeps on the floor
rolls. Somebody had unbuttoned

here we all are, strange air. Try
the Windsor knot in your tie,

but you will die by smashing
degraded and trembling,

that's why we practice dancing
to get used to being so close

to do it, to crash through
trash? When I hold up

you're small, only inches
and already halfway gone,

glass on the strip-edged
as if already in the presence

but a bad ping-pong ball,
way too often. Hunchbacked

pit, it rises in the west, races
in the east, two or three times

named for phobia. No, named
1877. *Phobos*—its name, like yours,

to somebody, or did once, now
nobody reads anymore page 127

summons Deimos and Phobos,
still dread dying? Fear it? Hardly

spoke in empires: a manifest
his math teacher, the fellow

Brigham Young had just died,
in newspapers had died in prison,

yesterday. You were alive then give
no, you were starlight and vodka.

by the bed. Coffee in the morning,
something on somebody and then

thinking about something else—
your plush new socks. Phobos, sorry

into the parent, but so will we all,
asking for one more day. Maybe

by standing on their shoes,
yet still in love. Will it hurt

Mother's teeth and become black
my hand to measure your face,

off the horizon, racing past us
the water in my jelly jar drinking

Formica tabletop trembling
of some new and eager god.

2. Demos

Begin

just before the Prado unveils a second *Mona Lisa*
covered since 1750 in bad varnish and black paint,
and just before another JPL dune buggy climbs past
my head on its way to Mars, I go to plot 4362, section 28,
to tell my parents about the craters on the second moon
of Mars, craters named for Swift and Voltaire, and I read
some Swift out loud to them while sitting on the Christmas
grass in my nice pants and a shirt with a buttoned collar,
mentioning as well how Swift wrote his own obituary and
that he worried about being a tree, alive but dead at the top,
and they answer for once and say, *Where's Amber*, meaning
my daughter, and I say, she couldn't make it, and *Where's
Fred*, meaning their other son, he's at church in Arizona,
Okay, is it nice out today, and I say, yes, you know it sort of is,
it is very nice today and I can see a black phoebe in its sooty
tuxedo vest catching something, day-flying moths I guess,
And so what about Voltaire, they say, and I say, not this time,
and you know, Mom, Dad, I need to tell you something,
there is something I need to tell you, and that is how sitting
here makes me feel like I weigh so much more than usual,
I don't know, it is like in this gravity I weigh hundreds
and hundreds of pounds, I can barely move, being here,
and I have to tell you something, I will not be back, not to
read with you about the moons, not any of it, so this is for
now I guess a sort of good-bye but that is it, good-bye

again.

Another Thing That Happened

Sometimes I like to go back and turn towns into glass and look down at my childhood
like the keeper of aquariums that I am, watching the people

sleeping, praying, enjoying the full 40-foot Bay of Fundy tides that are the emotions
after making love. How happy they look. How small and tidy.

There is the butcher's wife, hair henna'd red as new pennies, reading *The Godfather*,
page 27. There are the first Catholics I ever met,

twins. They made Lent sound like *lint*, what am I going to give up for *lint*,
and I did not know: my clothes were pretty good,

did not have much lint. That one must be Sandro, I remember him. The *abuelas*
all said he was the smart one. Not me—him.

He could finish his science homework plus mine in ten minutes before breakfast.
"When the universe was young,"

his report has started, "it was smaller, much hotter, and filled with a uniform glow
from its white-hot fog of hydrogen plasma."

That's no good. Time for an episode of *Vatos in Space*. One body dislodges another
and new moons careen

through the solar system and become new worlds, new possibilities. I will nudge Sandro
using my Tinker Bell wand. One, two, three *now*—

Sandro pauses, crosses out the beginning, starts again.

> *When I was young, I was smaller, much hotter, and filled with a uniform glow
> from the white-hot fog of my hydrogen plasma.*

Yes.

Journal Entry on the Way to Jupiter and Saturn

I remember when love was so abundant we whipsawed it

from ponds in midwinter to slab in sawdust until summer
or we taped it to knees following games of shirts and skins.

I remember how clear and smooth we salted it gone
from the driveway even while counting down inside

how long until we could hear the final small, after-dinner *clonk*
of it in a glass, and then the thin, socks-in-sawdust sound

of the children padding down the hallway. You took my hand
and pulled me after you.

Back to bed.

One of the Nicer Moons of Jupiter

Tomorrow probably it won't be, but right now it is
spring and ice thaws near a small house, hand built,

on a pale stone headland broomed by wind. I hurry to paint
the view before the wind skims the last ice from the pond.

In the barn, cattle wait to be fed; on the stove, milk scalds
the pan. In a back room, Rauschenberg erases de Kooning

again and again. Rothko is in the studio, smoking. Elsa
from the village has brought a basket to collect the laundry

but Sam Francis needs her to stand on a ladder, help stretch
more canvas. Andrew Wyeth scythes grass, ties it in bundles

to yellow. Which of us will cook dinner, round up the dog,
check to see that the mail came? There is always tomorrow.

Cy Twombly said today at breakfast, So am I dead? And
Johns reminded him, you won't be dead until we all agree,

and while you're working, it's easy to stay occupied,
put it off. *Think about it tomorrow*, we agreed. Until then,

the pines in this light shine like water, and somebody
should brush out the horses, and I have left my glasses

on the kitchen table, and I know I must hurry—we
all know this light won't last for very much longer.

The History of Jupiter 4 ("Callisto")

When they first settled on Callisto the whites killed the Indians and dumped their bodies in the geyser pools the only place to hide things but for years afterward the bodies kept coming back up, women, children, bodies, men, three one year, one the next, six the year after that, back up, bobbing back to the surface but coated with mineral crystals, the dead bodies of the first ones now completely covered in white and blue calcite, working headfirst back up to the surface to wait like tombstones or opal totem poles, what does it mean maybe nothing just a growing army of mineral people bearing witness and refusing to sit back down.

Saturn Times Saturn Divided by Saturn

I can remember when restaurants didn't have televisions I write in my notes, and then I step in and close the cage door again, go down Shaft 9 this time past the 5,000 foot marker. I get off at socks and lost children. Note the poison gas sensors, the guide tells me. Careful—mind your head. We call this chamber the Cascade of Tears. This one is Two Captains. To go deeper one needs more tokens, but even here, in our headlamp beams, doesn't the dust rise and billow like a lovely sort of curtain? Even here, couldn't you just reach out and touch them, both of your parents, but no, don't try, it's just the light hitting the dust, and come on, before you get your shirt cuffs dirty. They don't want to talk to you, and anyway, you've seen enough for now. Hear those bells? Three short, one long: time to go back up.

Lassell of Bolton Discovers Triton

Lassell

of Bolton

made his fortune

selling Liverpool beer, used

that money to make more money,

used *that* money to make telescopes bigger

and bigger each year, finding Triton a bright moon

of Neptune in 1846 just three weeks after Neptune itself

had just been found by the Germans. He was a favorite of

Queen Victoria, was father to a famous football striker. What

Mr. Lassell didn't know was that Triton's citizens had telepathy,

could know that he was watching, and so on the day itself

even the poorest and least interested of them

had put on something nice, a hat or a nice

scarf, had come into the main square,

and at the exact moment all the

people shouted and banged

pans, and even the babies

looked up smiling

and waved

at us.

Neptune 7 ("Larissa")

Each moon of Neptune differs from the next as much as your feet
differ from your shoes. Are as different from each other as ex–beauty

queens in their forties—some drinking too much, others still jaunty
on the fairway. As different as the kinds of cowries like broken mouths

in the basket of seashells in the gift shop in Waikiki. Put the shell
to your ear, you can hear Larissa talking, she is saying soon we will

be bone and ash no soon we will be sediment in a great sea no soon
that sea will drain away we will be a grain of amber rock locked in a

cabinet with a label that says 100 million years ago dinosaurs took mud
baths in this rock no soon the cabinet will be lost to a fire when the city

is abandoned in a radiation accident and the ash will lift on the wind
and the wind will lift on the sky and the sky will peel off into small thin flakes

like the scales of a butterfly no like the sides of a snowflake no like a micro-
meteorite a tenth of a tenth of a millimeter across, racing away from the sun

on a great explosion of solar wind and the micrometeorite has passed Venus
passed the Earth passed Saturn and Uranus, passed hundreds of moons, has

passed rings and shepherds and ended up here, on our glove, glowing under
a hand lens on the midnight side of S/1989 N 2, also called Moon 7 or Larissa,

also called who cares and what a doozy, also called the final resting place of
micrometeorite 7783391 as we slide it into a Lucite collection vial and write

down the grid numbers, one very very small piece of a diamond that has spent
two or three million years leaving the sun and pushing past all the meadows

and craters and shield volcano basalt flood plains to end up here, in our pocket,
and as the solution to the riddle goes, how do you find a needle in a haystack,

the answer is, you set fire to the hay and sift the ashes with a metal detector,
and that is what is called writing the history of the world now isn't it?

Voyager I Passes the Edge of the Solar System

Dimmer than a dirty
medium

far-off galaxy,
Voyager

waits for us
to catch up

just past the
heliopause,

the way that we each
one day will wait

for the nurse to come
and change the sheets

or push an amp of apple juice
into our mouths. We had so

much riding on Passing Fancy
in the sixth. Now we just want

to pass water or be able to read
ten pages without stopping.

If you want to make hand puppets
how many buttons will you need

to steal from the laundry;
if you want to hover in midair,

how long should you wait after
lights out. What is velocity × mass

minus your childhood? If you want
to go back and start over, it's a long walk,

not that far but far enough,
time to put on clean socks,

get started.

All philosophy is based on two things only:
curiosity and poor eyesight.

—BERNARD LE BOVIER DE FONTENELLE

NOTES

The section title "Invisible Terrain" comes from John Ashbery, "A Wave":

> *To pass through pain and not know it,*
> *A car door slamming in the night.*
> *To emerge on an invisible terrain.*

Jasper Johns about his dealers and collectors: "Artists are the elite of the servant class."

In "Somewhere Near the Rental Car Counter," the nineteenth-century botanist and naturalist Charles Wright (1811–85) is no relation to poet Charles Wright (1935–), other than they have the same name and the more recent Wright was once one of my teachers.

The quotation that ends "The History of Hell in America" appears in *The Wisdom of the Desert* by Thomas Merton, originally released in 1970 and happily still in print.

Bernard le Bovier de Fontenelle, author of the closing epigraph, lived to be one hundred, and when in his late nineties he met a beautiful young woman, he famously said, "Oh to be 80 again."

WISCONSIN POETRY SERIES

RONALD WALLACE, *Series Editor*

(B) = *Winner of the* **Brittingham Prize in Poetry**
(FP) = *Winner of the* **Felix Pollak Prize in Poetry**
(4L) = *Winner of the* **Four Lakes Prize in Poetry**

New Jersey **(B)** • Betsy Andrews

Salt **(B)** • Renée Ashley

Horizon Note **(B)** • Robin Behn

About Crows **(FP)** • Craig Blais

Mrs. Dumpty **(FP)** • Chana Bloch

The Declarable Future **(4L)** • Jennifer Boyden

The Mouths of Grazing Things **(B)** • Jennifer Boyden

Help Is on the Way **(4L)** • John Brehm

Sea of Faith **(B)** • John Brehm

Reunion **(FP)** • Fleda Brown

Brief Landing on the Earth's Surface **(B)** • Juanita Brunk

Ejo: Poems, Rwanda, 1991–1994 **(FP)** • Derick Burleson

Jagged with Love **(B)** • Susanna Childress

Almost Nothing to Be Scared Of **(4L)** • David Clewell

The Low End of Higher Things • David Clewell

Now We're Getting Somewhere **(FP)** • David Clewell

Taken Somehow by Surprise **(FP)** • David Clewell

Borrowed Dress **(FP)** • Cathy Colman

Places/Everyone **(B)** • Jim Daniels

Show and Tell • Jim Daniels

Darkroom **(B)** • Jazzy Danziger

And Her Soul Out of Nothing **(B)** • Olena Kalytiak Davis

My Favorite Tyrants **(B)** • Joanne Diaz

Talking to Strangers **(B)** • Patricia Dobler

Immortality **(FP)** • Alan Feldman

A Sail to Great Island **(FP)** • Alan Feldman

A Field Guide to the Heavens **(B)** • Frank X. Gaspar

The Royal Baker's Daughter **(FP)** • Barbara Goldberg

Funny **(FP)** • Jennifer Michael Hecht

The Legend of Light **(FP)** • Bob Hicok

Sweet Ruin **(B)** • Tony Hoagland

Partially Excited States **(FP)** • Charles Hood

Ripe **(FP)** • Roy Jacobstein

Saving the Young Men of Vienna **(B)** • David Kirby

Falling Brick Kills Local Man **(FP)** • Mark Kraushaar

Last Seen **(FP)** • Jacqueline Jones LaMon

The Lightning That Strikes the Neighbors' House **(4L)** • Nick Lantz

You, Beast **(B)** • Nick Lantz

The Unbeliever **(B)** • Lisa Lewis

Slow Joy **(B)** • Stephanie Marlis

Acts of Contortion **(B)** • Anna George Meek

Bardo **(B)** • Suzanne Paola

Meditations on Rising and Falling **(B)** • Philip Pardi

Old and New Testaments **(B)** • Lynn Powell

A Path between Houses **(B)** • Greg Rappleye

The Book of Hulga **(FP)** • Rita Mae Reese

Don't Explain **(FP)** • Betsy Sholl

Late Psalm • Betsy Sholl

Otherwise Unseeable **(4L)** • Betsy Sholl

Blood Work **(FP)** • Matthew Siegel

The Year We Studied Women **(FP)** • Bruce Snider

Bird Skin Coat **(B)** • Angela Sorby

The Sleeve Waves **(FP)** • Angela Sorby

Wait **(B)** • Alison Stine

Hive **(B)** • Christina Stoddard

The Red Virgin: A Poem of Simone Weil **(B)** • Stephanie Strickland

The Room Where I Was Born **(B)** • Brian Teare

Fragments in Us: Recent and Earlier Poems **(FP)** • Dennis Trudell

The Apollonia Poems **(4L)** • Judith Vollmer

Level Green **(B)** • Judith Vollmer

Reactor • Judith Vollmer

Voodoo Inverso **(FP)** • Mark Wagenaar

Hot Popsicles • Charles Harper Webb

Liver **(FP)** • Charles Harper Webb

The Blue Hour **(B)** • Jennifer Whitaker

Centaur **(B)** • Greg Wrenn

Pocket Sundial **(B)** • isa Zeidner